So…You Think You Want to **Speak** in Dentistry?

Vanessa Emerson

Founder, Dental Speaker Institute
& Dental Speakers Bureau

The Dental
Speaker

What's Inside?

This book is for YOU if....

- You are a dental professional with years of industry specific knowledge and experience.

- You've mastered your craft and feel pulled to share your knowledge with others via the speaking platform, consulting, or another method of teaching.

- You, like most aspiring and developing dental speakers, are seeking guidance in what to do (and not do) to he p you find the shortcuts to success.

Speaking in the dental industry can be a personally and professionally satisfying and financially rewarding career choice. However, it does take *time, work and a financial investment* to develop the essential skills and marketing materials to get your business up and keep it running.

Dive into this meaty *how-to* guide to learn if dental speaking may be the right fit for you!

Introduction

Growing up in a small farming community in northeastern Arizona in the 1970's, I learned the value of systems, processes and hard work.

My family raised a large garden each year. Dad planted trees to create an orchard. We raised chickens, rabbits, goats, and there was usually a cow or a horse in the back pasture. And, of course, there were always dogs and cats.

Our environment and experience shape us.

Flash forward to today. For the past 20 years, this farm girl has worked to support dental speakers and consultants. I believe that you are reading this book because you have grown to a point in your career where you feel that you have something to give back. There is something that you learned that has helped you, you have mastered it and now have a desire to help others by sharing this knowledge.

*Your environment and experience has shaped **you**.*
Would you agree?

Growing up on a farm taught me about the importance of having a vision, a plan and taking action.

For instance, growing a successful garden requires these three. We do not just throw out seeds and hope we end up with a harvest. Similarly, we don't plant seeds and dig them up and eat them because it's taking too long for the food to grow.

A business - whether a dental practice or a consultancy – is like a garden in that it is strategically planned. It is grown. It is tended.

With his vision in mind, Dad created a strategy and had a plan for action every year. His vision: a harvest that would last for months, feed his family of seven with enough excess to share with neighbors in the community, as well as can, freeze and store what was left for the rest of the year.

First, he would rototill the land. Then he would painstakingly and back-breakingly create long, perfect rows. Those rows must be absolutely straight to channel the water through the garden on irrigation day. If the row was not straight, the water would quickly erode the row and all of his hard work would literally wash away. I recall Dad planting a small stake at the end of each row and running a string between those stakes. He would bend down on one knee and look down the row to ensure the row lined up perfectly with the string. And if it was not perfectly straight, he would grab the hoe and make it so.

Seeds would be planted. Weeds would be hoed or pulled by hand. Irrigation would occur at regular, consistent intervals. Plants would be thinned out. Pests would be organically disposed of. And in due time, the harvest would begin.

Similar y, there are multiple steps and processes for starting and growing a speaking business. Just like the garden, when these systems are followed one will usually obtain the desired outcome – the harvest – which is business success. In this book, we will examine a 3-part strategy for launching and growing a dental speaking and consulting business. It all starts with vision, strategy and taking action.

Before we dive in, let's clarify terminology. Speaking. Consulting. Mentoring. Coaching. Training. Seminar. Lecture. Keynote. And the list goes on. These are all varying shades of the same activity: educating an audience (whether it be an audience of 1 or 1,000). Speaking and consulting activities are similar in nature and dovetail/overlap in many ways. For the purpose of this book, I will refer to speaking primarily. Know that the information that follows generally also applies to each of these other terms.

Speaking and consulting can be both personally and professionally fulfilling and profitable. There are different paths that dental professionals take. Below are a few of the more popular business models:

- Many dental professionals expand their careers to include these services while remaining full or part time in the dental practice.
- Some professionals move in this direction as they near their exit from clinical practice.
- Some will opt to grow a full time speaking and consulting business.

Note: It's not necessary to have worked in the dental practice to speak in dentistry. Many speakers without dental practice experience bring valuable knowledge to the industry.

In this book, I will be sharing ideas and methods that have worked for me and my clients. My objective is to give you a solid understanding of what it takes to start and grow this business and with this knowledge you can determine the path that will work best for you and your situation.

Exercise:

1) What are some of the qualities that you appreciate in really good speakers?

2) What is it about speaking/consulting that attracts you? Why do you feel drawn to it?

3) What is holding you back? What is a roadblock that you'd like some clarity around? What about speaking/consulting worries you?

4) What do you most want to know about becoming a speaker or consultant?

Part 1

The Business of Speaking

*"If you don't know where you are going,
any road will get you there."*

Cheshire Cat; Alice in Wonderland

Create a business that supports and ALIGNS with your Life Vision.

I have childhood memories of mornings where I'm heading to the kitchen looking for breakfast. I know mom is near because breakfast is in the process of becoming. I invariably would find her on the carport, checking in on her outside kitties. She gave them boxes with blankets and shelter. She would feed and care for them. There were no animals in our house because my father was allergic. Yet, there are animals everywhere on the farm. And mom always had cats. Our yard was shelter for any stray feline. So, it's likely mom's fault that I'm a cat lady.

Or, it could have been Grandma Jewel. I remember sleepovers at Grandma's house. I was about 5 years old. I recall her telling me stories, singing songs, rubbing my back before we slept. The bed felt so big compared to my bunk bed. Large enough for both her dog and cat to sleep with us! Her beautiful Siamese cuddled up next to my leg the whole night. *A cat. Inside. On the bed!* So, it may have all started with Grandma Jewel.

Our environment and experience shape us.

I now live in the Phoenix area where the Humane

Society estimates that there are over a quarter of a million free roaming cats in our communities. That's 250,000 cats living outdoors.

I actually became a cat *activist* eight years ago. That summer, while walking my dobie, we found two separate litters of kittens in our community. I brought food and water for them daily. By the time he was about five months old, I finally figured out how to catch and bring home Einstein: a black and white tuxedo cat with white hair growing wildly out of his ears. Einie was our first rescue. We have since helped nearly 50 cats that have been adopted out, trapped-neutered-and-returned to our community (TNR), or – my personal favorite - foster "failed". My husband, Jeff, and I operate an amateur cat rescue and sanctuary from our home where we typically house around a dozen indoor cats, a handful of backyard cats, and feed and care for the free roaming cats within our community in cooperation with our home owner's association.

Understanding that the success of my business is directly tied to my ability to care for more community cats gives me a push to get up in the morning. The more profitable my business, the more cats we are able to help.

What... for *YOU*... is *CATS* for me?

If you've not yet thought out or written down your LIFE vision or if it's been some time since you've done this exercise, this will be your starting place. Locking in on a life vision that fuels your fire is step one. Next you will build a business strategy to support and align with that life vision. More on strategy in the next section. Let's get clear about your life vision before we go any further.

When I did this personal work several years ago, I utilized an exercise from a wonderful business book: <u>Making Money is Killing Your Business</u> (Blakeman). About 1/3 of the way into this 'must read' business guide, author Chuck Blakeman's vision exercise will help you gain clarity and create a written vision that should be kept near you for ease of reference. I've carried my life vision in my wallet for years. It is also in my strategic plan.

Somewhere in years past I stumbled across a fun exercise that would also help you get this process started. Jeff and I enjoy taking long hikes near our home in the Phoenix area. Some hikes last four to five hours. Conversation can dwindle. That's when he or I will pop the question:

"What did you do with your billion dollars today?"

If money were truly of no concern, how would you live out your day to day existence? What activities, causes, and passions would you pursue? Specifically, how would you spend your time and exactly what would you do with your days?

Example: My Life Vision

I choose a simple, happy, relaxed life and make time to enjoy the beauty and joy around me. I spend my days in a blend of love, work and play, with plenty of exercise and a flexible schedule. It FEELS present, peaceful, confident, happy, energizing, joyful and loving.

Ideal Lifestyle:
- Continued spiritual refinement and personal growth
- Time with family and friends
- Animals and nature – exercise – daily meditation
- Help operate an outdoor cat rescue in Phoenix area
- Abundant relationships, finances, health, and spirituality

Exercise:

Invest the time and soul searching *now* to determine the LIFE goals that your business will support.

The internet is overflowing with life vision exercises. I've included a few options in Appendix I at the back of this book.

If you are not sure about your life vision exactly, jot down what you think you might want to do, be, and have. Where do you think you'd like to be in 3, 5, 10 years. What do you do with your days? How do you spend your time?

My Life Vision

Do:

Be:

Have:

Develop a Strategic Plan

The Strategic Plan is a blueprint for your business development and connects your LIFE VISION to your BUSINESS VISION.

Picture a stool with multiple legs supporting it. The legs all work together to support the overall structure. This is similar in concept to our strategic plan. Now think of each stool leg as a profit center for the business.

What are some of the profit centers you might see in a speaking/consulting business? Below are a few examples.
- Speaking
  - Be hired to speak at someone's meeting
  - Speak at your own self-sponsored meeting
  - Speak virtually via screen share
- Consulting
  - In-office, over the phone or virtual/remote
  - Mentoring, coaching, training
- Product Sales
  - Books
  - Software
  - Training videos
  - Forms
- Online Educational Offerings

Exercise:
Turn to Appendix II at the back of this book.

Now let's assign the profit centers (legs of your stool) to your strategic plan. *Keep it high level for now* and just fill in the first level. Will you speak and consult? Do you already know that you'd like to create product(s)?

As we make our way through Parts 2 and 3 of our Strategy for Success, be listening through the filter of:
- How does this apply to my business?
- Do I want to explore this idea further? Or add it to my plan?
-

For right now, we're just capturing thoughts. Just jot it down. We will circle back around and flesh the plan out more.

Strategic Plan Example:

Speaking
1) Join Toastmasters by Jan 15
2) Draft speech outline (February)
3) Create website by Mar 31

Consulting
1) Contact local society for list of dentists – this week
2) Attend "Train the Trainer" workshop (May 14-15)
3) Create marketing flyer by Feb 15 – contact designer

Product Sales
1) Finish book draft by end of January
2) Research Amazon publishing guidelines – Feb 15
3) Learn how to add online CE content – attend webinar Apr 17

Part 2

Build Your Speech and Skills

*"Be an original voice,
not an annoying echo."*

Simon Bailey

Determine / Uncover Your Niche

You would not be reading this book if you did not have something to share. There is something pulling you here. Something that the world needs to hear. Are you already clear what that speaking or consulting topic is?

Think about what you want to speak about and why. Why are you drawn to speaking and consulting? What topic or audience demographic do you feel pulled toward?

This is another area where environment and experience has shaped us. Determining your niche starts with self-reflection and an analysis of your *skill sets, experiences and knowledge.*

Don't go after a niche because you think it will be popular. Rather, brand yourself in a topic area because you are actually an expert in that topic area. Lean into your own personal experience. What professional topic are you passionate about? Where do you have deep knowledge to share? What have you mastered?

Exercise:

To *start* the process of defining your niche, please consider - then answer - the following questions:

1. In what topic area(s) do I have deep experience and have mastered skills?

2. What specialized (target) market could I serve?

3. What could I specialize in?

4. What products and/or services could I offer?

5. Why would people want to buy from me?

6. What do I want others to know and say about my products or services?

Develop Your Content

Move your thoughts from your head to your computer where you can more easily work with them and start developing your content.

Start by capturing your thoughts in a digital form. This can be an audio recording or a Word document. As you think about what you would like to teach, organize your notes and file the stories and teaching points so you can refer easily to them.

Then, start small.   You don't have to write a full day speech immediately! In fact, you don't have to create a full day speech at all.

Start by creating blog articles for your website. The typical blog article is 400 – 700 words. Don't try to cover more than one teaching point in this short article. For instance, create a top 10 list in your topic area: ways to market a practice, tips on how to brush and floss, steps for creating a paperless practice, etc.

Other small projects to help you get started:
- Write for industry publications.
- Be a guest on dental podcasts, webinars, teleseminars, and Facebook LIVE sessions.
- Write a book! There is no minimum page or size requirement.

- Create online educational courses. This can be as straight forward as creating an hour of content, video recording on your computer with a screen sharing software such as Zoom, and uploading that video to an online education platform.

Bottom line: *Just get started!* Whether you write, voice record or video record, start getting your thoughts from your head to your computer so your content can be crafted into something greater.

Exercise:
Refer back to your Strategic Plan (Appendix II). Add the following task to the plan: Get your content into a digital form, i.e., write a blog article, participate on a podcast, etc. Assign a due date.

Improve Your Presentation and Training Skills

All speakers benefit from training in the area of content development and presentation skills. There are many exceptional workshops and one-on-one coaching opportunities available to help you develop your skills.

Dental Speaker Institute (DSI) offers a mastery program for the dental speaker and an opportunity to earn the Professional Dental Speaker (PDS) designation. DSI has assembled and vetted a comprehensive group of speaker development experts who provide exceptional training programs in the art, craft and business of speaking.

Turn to Appendix III to view a list of trusted professional resources in this area. Or visit www.DentalSpeakerInstitute.com/faculty to connect with these experts and their training options.

Build Relationships/Network

Your social network provides the opportunity to accomplish together what would be difficult or impossible for individuals to accomplish alone.

> If you want to go fast, go alone.
> If you want to go far, go together.
> *African Proverb*

I've read (and re-read a couple of times) a fabulous book about the importance and benefits of building strong relationships with other professionals.

In her book, "How to be a Power Connector", Judy Robinett claims:

> "In any conference, meeting or group
> of 10 or more people,
> the solution to any problem is in the room."

That's a pretty big claim! And one that we put to the test during an Academy of Dental Management Consultants annual session. When speaking on the topic of networking, I engaged the attendees in an exercise to test this theory. After only a few minutes of conversation with a new contact, the majority of the room reported that they had already found a likely solution to a business challenge. We felt that this had proved the theory to be accurate.

The more that you network, participate and build relationships, the more opportunity that will be presented. In Appendix IV, I share a list of the organizations through which membership would help you grow your dental speaking business.

The best way to build your network is to put yourself in places where you can get to know people personally. Before you attend a conference or meeting, determine what you hope to achieve by attending and *figure out how to help others BEFORE you ask them for something*. You may have connections that would be helpful to a colleague. You may be able to serve on a committee. Or know of a great speaker for a future meeting. You may be able to mentor a young colleague. How can you give back to others in the organization?

A successful new contact relationship building conversation will include these elements:

- Connect personally (ask them about themselves)
- Connect professionally (ask them about their work)
- And ask Judy Robinett's Three Golden Questions:
    1) How can I help you?
    2) What ideas do you have for me?
    3) Who do you know that I should talk to?

By utilizing this formula in our exercise at the ADMC annual session, our meeting attendees were able to zero in to their answers within a few minutes. Utilize the formula to grow your circle of influence and create a greater impact in the industry.

Turn to Appendix IV for a list of organizations with programs geared specifically for speakers.

Exercise:

Refer back to your Strategic Plan (Appendix II). Under each leg of your stool (profit center), write in your ideas for projects, tasks and action items as they relate to this section.

Specifically, what is your next step for:
- Determining your niche?
- Developing your content?
- Increasing your skills?
- How will you increase your networking opportunities?

Part 3

Get Booked

*"Your best marketing tool is
an exceptional presentation."*

Vanessa Emerson

You know what you want to speak about. You are developing your content and skill. *Now, you need clients.* You need to create a buzz around your presentations and you need to get them in front of meeting planners. *You need to market.*

The very best way for you to get booked is to present an exceptional speech. You'll know it's exceptional because it spins off business (more speaking opportunities, consulting clients, product sales, etc.) Until you are receiving spin off business from *every* presentation you give, you know that you need to continue to refine your message and polish your presentation skills.

The challenge that is inherent in the above paragraph is getting booked in the first place so you can give that excellent speech. You'll need to start pushing your marketing efforts forward and as you build some momentum, the speaking engagements will start being booked and eventually (usually after a few years) you can ease up a little on your marketing efforts. However, to keep one's speaking calendar and pipeline full, a savvy speaker will continually market even when the calendar is full.

Let's take a look at a foundational marketing campaign. The ground level.

Foundational Marketing Materials

A few tips that apply across all marketing mediums:

Give some thought to your brand, which includes your logo, colors and the look/feel of your materials overall. See **Appendix I** for exercises to help you determine your branding and differentiation.

If you'd like help, email
nfo@TheDentalSpeaker.com

Whether you're writing a course description, an article or a webpage, it is important to include the following elements:

- What is the pain/problem/challenge
    - What keeps them up at night?
- Show how you resolve that challenge with this course, article, etc.
    - What exactly is taught during the course?
- Why you? How do you differentiate?
    - What is it about the way you teach the course; or what skills, experience or training that you bring makes you different / stand out?

Additionally, make sure that your materials appeal to the attendee by talking about what's in it for them.   For instance, don't start your packet with your bio. Start with the challenge that your target audience member is having and then show how your course resolves it. The bio comes later in the packet.

Speaker Packet

Let's look at the design of a speaker's marketing materials sometimes called a *one sheet, speaker packet or speaker materials.*

A speaker packet is the foundation of a speaker's marketing program. Everything else builds from the work you'll do creating your speaker packet, i.e., website, email campaign, mail campaigns, etc. The speaker packet contains the following elements:

- Cover
- Summary (if you have 2 or more courses)
- Course Description(s)
    - One page per course
    - Your photo and contact info
    - Clearly defined synopsis & objectives
- Bio
- Past presentations
- Testimonials

The purpose of the speaker packet is to detail and promote your presentation offerings, establish you as an expert, clearly show how your presentations differentiate and get you booked.

Where to Start?

I suggest gathering ideas by looking at other speaker's materials. *I do not advocate copying others' work* We gain creative ideas by looking at examples of what we are trying to accomplish. A few options:

- Examples of Speaker Packets are available in the "Portfolio' section of our website: **TheDentalSpeaker.com/speakermarketing**
- Visit online directories, such as
  - DentalSpeakersBureau.com
  - DentalSpeakerInstitute.com
- Check out the websites of other speakers. Most established speakers will make their speaker materials available online.
- Share your ideas for materials with your colleagues – *start a mastermind group!*

My advice is to *just start*! Start writing your copy. If you don't have the perfect photo, title, etc., use what you have. As is true with your website, your speaker marketing materials will be updated and modified frequently.

Website

Every speaker must have a web presence in order to be found in today's dental speaking environment. Either create a speaker (and consultant) website or add a "seminars" or "speaking" menu item to your dental practice site.

The meeting planner is most likely going to google your name when you are referred to them. They will want to find you online and learn about your courses before they contact you. Make it easy for them. Create a web presence and ensure your speaker packet is included there.

- For speaker website examples, visit **TheDentalSpeaker.com/speakermarketing**

Email and Print Campaigns

Email marketing is a low cost, easy way to maintain an ongoing presence with meeting planners. To get the best results, make a phone call to the planners that "click through" on your campaign. Visit your email service dashboard to view your campaign results and determine which of your contacts wanted to learn more by "clicking" through on your campaign.

We've seen the popularity of print marketing fade and then resurge in recent years.   A targeted postcard marketing campaign is low cost, low risk and can bring you results.

The best mail and email list will always be one that you've built over time with your own opted-in contacts. As you work to build your customized contact list, know that meeting planner contacts are usually easily accessible through an organization's' website.   Dental meeting planner lists are available at www.TheDentalSpeaker.com.

Directories and Bureaus

A directory is similar to the yellow pages and white pages from yesteryear. With a directory, you can find a speaker by searching for their name or their speaking topic.

A speakers bureau is a higher level of service. A bureau will help the planner find the speaker that is the right fit for their meeting.

Example: www.DentalSpeakersBureau.com combines the directory and bureau into one site.

Thought Leadership

Establishing yourself as a leader in thought (a key opinion leader) is the next step once you've established your foundational marketing campaign (previous steps in this chapter).

Thought leadership activities include the following:
- Have an active blog presence
- Write articles for industry publications
- Host your own or participate in others'
  - Webinars
  - Podcasts
  - Facebook LIVE
  - Teleseminars
- Write a book
- Create online educational courses
- ... and more!

Outsource

For the same reason you hire a contractor or mechanic to make repairs, outsource your administrative and marketing projects to experts who know the industry. It will save you time, money and frustration in the long run.

Exercise:

Refer back to your Strategic Plan (Appendix II).
Under each leg of your stool (profit center), write
in your ideas for projects, tasks and action items as
they relate to this section.

Specifically, what is your next step for:
- Creating your speaker packet
- Developing a strong, effective web presence
- Planning your ongoing marketing campaign
- Listing with online directories/bureaus
- Engaging in Thought Leadership activities

In Closing

"Every ending is a new beginning."

Marianne Williamson

Ready to Begin?

Reach out to industry consultants and speakers to ask for advice. Look for a mentor. You'll find that dentistry is brimming with abundance-minded professionals who care and share, and who understand that together we can create a greater positive impact in the industry.

Work one-on-one with a coach. Work with more than one coach. The bottom line is that you'll achieve your results faster when you work with someone who has been there, done that, and that works with others who want to replicate those results.

Allow the process to unfold naturally, step by step. Do one thing today to move toward your goals. Don't let analysis paralysis take hold! Don't wait until your content and skills and marketing materials are perfect. *Just take that one next step.*

Exercise:
Refer back to your Strategic Plan (Appendix II). Under each leg of your stool (profit center), prioritize and assign a target (due) date for each of the projects, tasks and action items you've entered.

This is a living document that will continuously change. Keep it near your computer and refer to it often.

I encourage you to commit today to the following:

- What will you STOP DOING in order to move forward?
    - Stop waiting for it to be perfect?
    - Stop procrastinating?
- What will you START DOING to move forward?
    - Request to work one day less each week to give you time to develop your speaking business?
    - Determine your brand or your message?
- What will you COMMIT TO DO in the next week to help you grow the garden of your speaking/consulting business?
    - Review your strategic plan and determine one item that is a MUST DO this week. Then do it!

We started this journey together by highlighting the importance of systems, processes and hard work. Whether it be on the farm or in your speaking business, these are essential for finding success.

We've identified the steps for launching and growing this business and with this knowledge you can better determine the path that will work for you and your situation.

The first step is to ensure you are clear about your life vision and where you are hoping to end up. I shared with you a little about my passion for helping community cats. I'd like to leave you with this thought which will give you a glimpse into one of my major life goals.

I would like to be a member of a team that brings an outdoor cat sanctuary to the Phoenix area. An outdoor sanctuary can help many more animals than we can help through our indoor rescues.

There are a few examples of this type of outdoor sanctuary:

- CatHouseOnTheKings.com
- LanaiCatSanctuary.com

My goals, my purpose, and my life vision involves helping community cats on a grand scale. One that can make a significant impact on the lives of the 250,000 free roaming cats that must find a way to survive on the streets of the Phoenix area. *This vision fuels my desire to build a stronger, more profitable business.* It helps me jump out of bed in the morning, excited for another work day.

What... for YOU... is *CATS* for me?

Let that *vision and passion* be the fuel that feeds your internal fire and propels your speaking and consulting business to great heights.

Appendices

"Don't let perfectionism keep you from getting started. Take that one next step."

Vanessa Emerson

Appendix I

Define Your Life Vision/Purpose

Your Life Vision can bring purpose and deeper meaning to your business and life. It is something you plug into emotionally that drives you during times of challenge. It's not a wish or a goal. The Life Vision can be felt with all of your soul and is something that for which no matter what happens you will make sure you stay the course.

Following are a few exercises designed to help you uncover or confirm your Live Vision.

Finding Your Ikigai: A Japanese Concept Meaning "A Reason for Being".

Draw four concentric circles that overlap in the middle. Label each circle as you see in the bullets below. Notate your answers to the questions below in their corresponding circle. Ikigai is the convergence of four primary elements (the space in the middle):

- What you Love (your passion)
- What the World Needs (your mission)
- What you are Good at (your vocation)
- What you can get Paid for (your profession)

Now write whatever words and ideas come up for you in each circle, then look for areas where they overlap. Reflect on the total of these elements and how they relate to each other. Your reason for being is that sweet spot in the middle. The place of joy.

Create a List

Start with a piece of paper and write down something you want. Then write WHY you want it. Continue to ask WHY and drill down until you feel empowered by the answer. Then write down the next thing that you want. Ask WHY. Rinse. Repeat.

It's not about finding something that inspires you. The purpose is to define YOUR reason to get out of bed and never quit, especially when times are tough.

Additional Resource:

Making Money is Killing Your Business; Chuck Blakeman; Chapter 6: The Single Most Important Question in Business.

Appendix II

Draft Your Strategic Plan

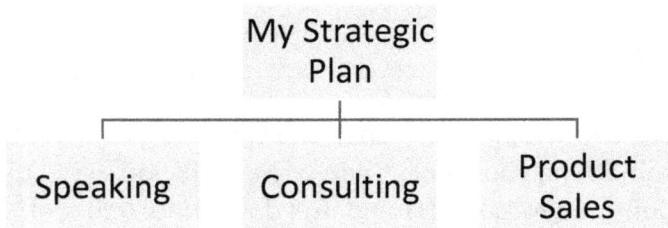

```
                    My Strategic
                        Plan
        ┌───────────────┼───────────────┐
    Speaking        Consulting        Product
                                       Sales
```

Appendix III

Build your Content Development, Presentation and Business Skills

ChuckBlakeman.com

DezThornton.com

JenniferSchultz.com

LaserPointerPresentations.com

LionSpeak.net

MarkLeBlanc.com

MinalSampat.com

PaulHomoly.com

TheDentalSpeaker.com

TheEleniGroup.com

TimGard.com

Appendix IV

Professional Organizations for the Dental Speaker/Consultant

TheDentalSpeaker.com
    Speaker Marketing and Business Guidance

DentalSpeakerInstitute.com
    Master's Program
    Professional Dental Speaker (PDS) Designation
    JUMPSTART Conferences

DentalSpeakersBureau.com
    Connecting Planners with Right Fit Speakers

Toastmasters.org
    Get Started Writing and Presenting Your Content

NSASpeaker.org
    Speaker Support Association (all industries)

ADMC.net
    Consultant Support Organization and Network

Appendix V
Brand & Differentiation Exercises

Between these two exercises, you will find **repetitive topics and ideas** which will help you put wording, graphics and emotion around your brand.

Defining Your Brand:

1. What niche does your company fill? What specialized market do you serve?

2. Who is your target market?

3. What are the core values of your company?

4. What is the mission/vision of your company?

5. What does your company specialize in?   Or would you like to specialize in?

6. What products and/or services do you offer? Or would like to offer?

7. Why do people want to buy from you?

8. What do you want your brand to do for your company?

9. What do you want others to know and say about your products or services?

10. What words do you think someone would use to describe your company?

Differentiation Exercise:

1. What do I want my audience to know, feel, believe, support?

2. Why is this information important to them, and why now?

3. What is the 'pain' around this subject?

4. How does my approach, idea, assertion address that pain?

5. What's new, different or enlightened about my take on this topic?

6. How do I ensure results or change behaviors with this presentation?

7. How do I differentiate as a presenter?

ABOUT THE AUTHOR

Vanessa Emerson helps event planners and educators find and work with each other.

Founder of Dental Speaker Institute and Dental Speakers Bureau, Vanessa Emerson is known as a thought leader by clients, prospects, meeting planners and peers. Her marketing services are in high demand, specializing in speaker materials, website design and e-mail marketing services.

A member of Academy of Dental Management Consultants since 2013, Vanessa is honored to serve as co-chair of the Academy's Marketing Committee.

Honored by Dental Products Report as one of the Top 25 Women in Dentistry (2017), Vanessa is known as the 'go to' resource for inside-the-industry information that helps meeting planners create better meetings, speakers acquire more bookings and BOTH to meet their business goals. She is frequently booked by dental organizations who would like to encourage their members to explore and expand their roles as speakers and consultants in dentistry.